MAR 2 0

Shark Bites

Angel Shark

by Jenna Lee Gleisner

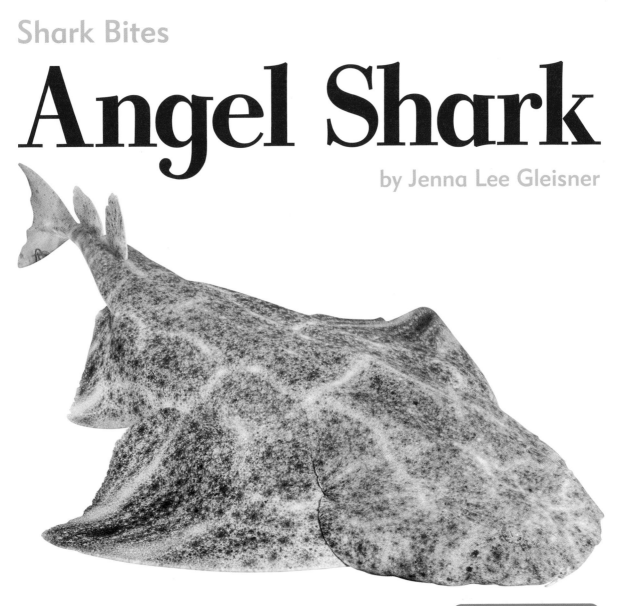

Ideas for Parents and Teachers

Bullfrog Books let children practice reading informational text at the earliest reading levels. Repetition, familiar words, and photo labels support early readers.

Before Reading

- Discuss the cover photo. What does it tell them?

- Look at the picture glossary together. Read and discuss the words.

Read the Book

- "Walk" through the book and look at the photos. Let the child ask questions. Point out the photo labels.

- Read the book to the child, or have him or her read independently.

After Reading

- Prompt the child to think more. Ask: Angel sharks look like rays. Can you think of other animals that look similar to one another?

Bullfrog Books are published by Jump!
5357 Penn Avenue South
Minneapolis, MN 55419
www.jumplibrary.com

Library of Congress Cataloging-in-Publication Data

Names: Gleisner, Jenna Lee, author.
Title: Angel shark / by Jenna Lee Gleisner.
Description: Bullfrog books edition. Minneapolis, MN: Jump!, Inc., [2020]
Series: Shark bites
Includes bibliographical references and index.
Audience: Age 5-8. | Audience: K to Grade 3.
Identifiers: LCCN 2019001172 (print)
LCCN 2019002849 (ebook)
ISBN 9781641289566 (ebook)
ISBN 9781641289559 (hardcover : alk. paper)
Subjects: LCSH: Squatinidae—Juvenile literature.
Classification: LCC QL638.95.S88 (ebook)
LCC QL638.95.S88 G54 2020 (print)
DDC 597.3—dc23
LC record available at https://lccn.loc.gov/2019001172

Editors: Susanne Bushman and Jenna Trnka
Design: Shoreline Publishing Group

Photo Credits: Martin Voeller/iStock, cover; Kelvin Aitken/VWPics/Alamy, 1; Biosphoto/Alamy, 3; Luis Miguel Estevez/Dreamstime, 4, 5, 18–19, 20–21, 23br; Luis Miguel Estevez/Shutterstock, 6–7, 10–11, 23tl; Carlost Villoch/MagicSea/Alamy, 8; Shaun Wilkinson/Shutterstock, 9; Paulo Oliveiro/Alamy, 12, 23bl; David Fleetham/Alamy, 13; Stephen Wong & Takako Uno, 14–15, 16–17, 23tr; Michael Wood/Dreamstime, 22; Olena Zaskochenko/Shutterstock, 24.

Printed in the United States of America at Corporate Graphics in North Mankato, Minnesota.

Table of Contents

Master of Disguise

Something is hiding.

Can you see it?

It is an angel shark!

Its body is flat.

It lies in the sand.

It blends in.

It is a small shark.

It is only six feet
(1.8 meters) long.

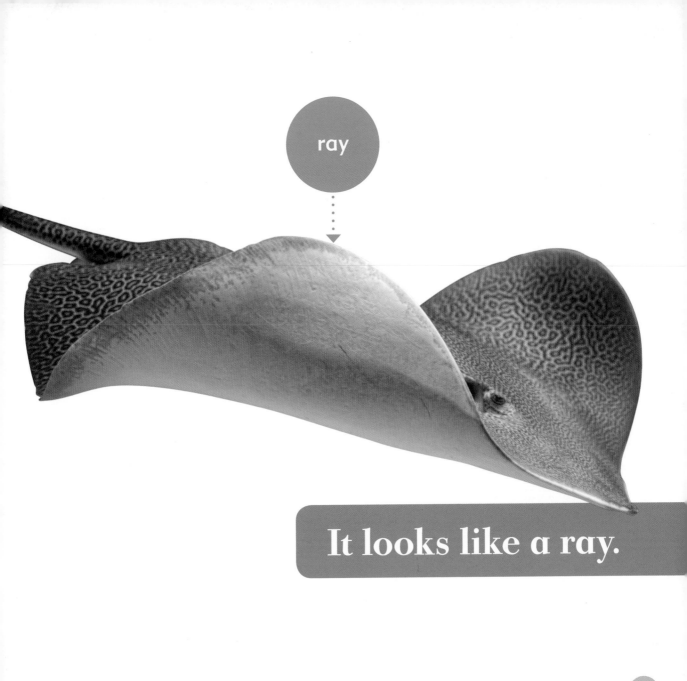

ray

It looks like a ray.

9

eye

Eyes are on top
of its head.

It watches.

It waits.

For what?

Food!

Here come fish.

The shark feels them.

How?

Barbels.

barbel

It lunges!
Wow!

It swallows its prey.
It eats it whole.
Yum!

It lives in shallow waters.

Why?

It is warm.

At night, it swims.

Nice!

The shark waits
during the day.

It buries itself
again.

It waits for food.

Parts of an Angel Shark

caudal fin
This tail fin helps an angel shark push off from the sand when attacking prey.

dorsal fin

body
Angel sharks have flat bodies. Their color helps them blend in with the seafloor.

pelvic fin

pectoral fins
Large, winglike pectoral fins make angel sharks look like rays.

eyes
Eyes are on top of an angel shark's head so it can watch for prey while buried in sand.

barbels
Barbels feel and taste prey.

Picture Glossary

blends in
Looks the same
as its surroundings.

lunges
Leaps or plunges
forward suddenly.

prey
Animals that are hunted
by other animals for food.

shallow
Not deep.

Index

To Learn More

Finding more information is as easy as 1, 2, 3.

❶ Go to www.factsurfer.com

❷ Enter "angelshark" into the search box.

❸ Choose your book to see a list of websites.